PIANO • VOCAL • GUITAR

VANCE J...

'dream your life away

2	WINDS OF CHANGE
7	MESS IS MINE
13	WASTED TIME
22	RIPTIDE
29	WHO AM I
34	FROM AFAR
41	WE ALL DIE TRYING TO GET IT RIGHT
48	GEORGIA
52	RED EYE
61	FIRST TIME
67	ALL I EVER WANTED
71	BEST THAT I CAN
78	MY KIND OF MAN
86	FIRE AND THE FLOOD
92	STRAIGHT INTO YOUR ARMS

ISBN 978-1-4950-5666-6

HAL•LEONARD®
CORPORATION
7777 W. BLUEMOUND RD. P.O. BOX 13819 MILWAUKEE, WI 53213

Visit Hal Leonard Online at
www.halleonard.com

WINDS OF CHANGE

Words and Music by
VANCE JOY

With energy

I miss you ___ more ___ than you could know.
reach out ___ for ___ me in the night

I

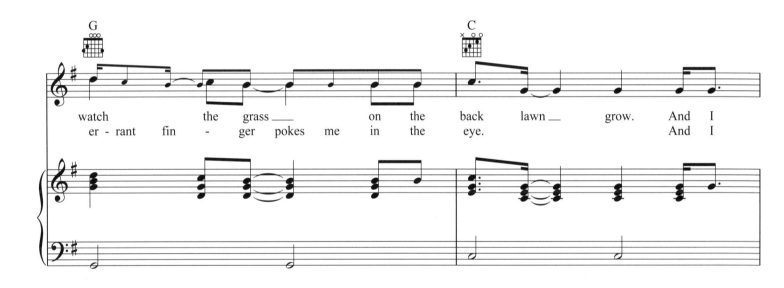

watch the grass ___ on the back lawn ___ grow. And I
er-rant fin-ger pokes me in the eye. And I

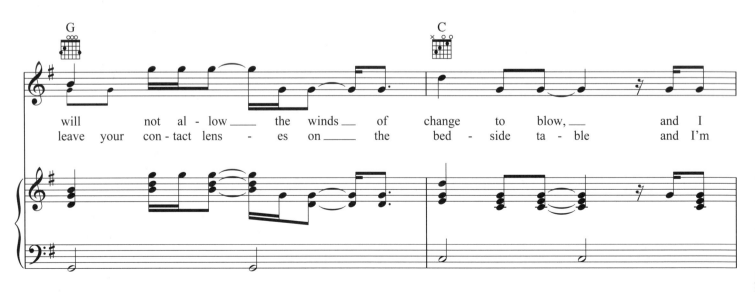

will not al-low ___ the winds ___ of change to blow, ___ and I
leave your con-tact lens-es on ___ the bed-side ta-ble and I'm

hope _____ you de - cide _____ to come back
hop - ing you de - cide _____ to come back

home.
home.
'Cause

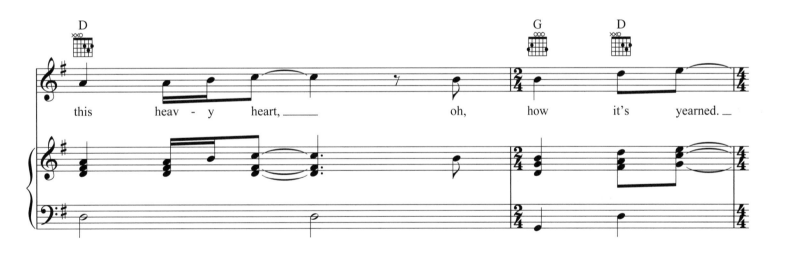

this heav - y heart, _____ oh, how it's yearned. _____

_____ 'Cause I've been a - lone _ far too _ long,

when are you ___ com - ing home, ___ my love? My

love. ___ You

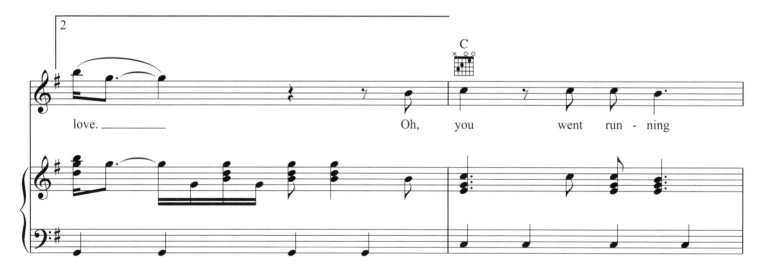

love. ___ Oh, you went run - ning

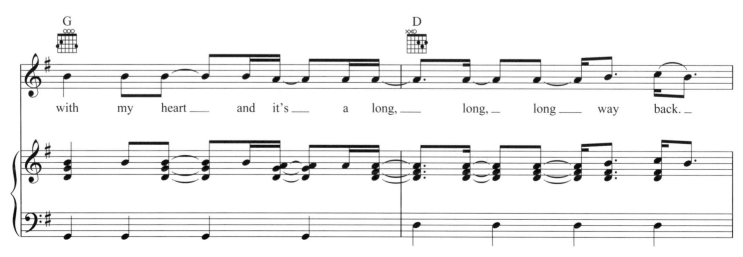

with my heart ___ and it's ___ a long, ___ long, ___ long ___ way back. ___

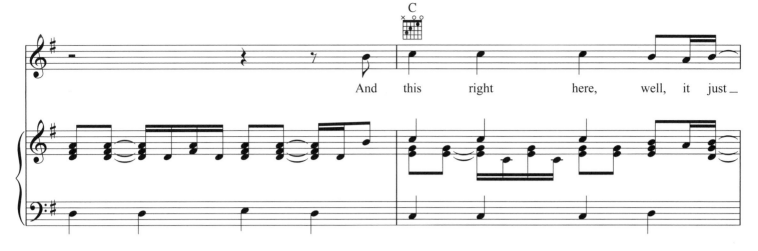

And this right here, well, it just __

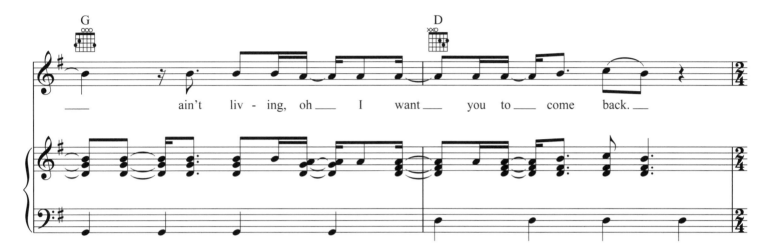

__ ain't liv- ing, oh __ I want __ you to __ come back. __

Well, I've been a- lone __ far too __ long,

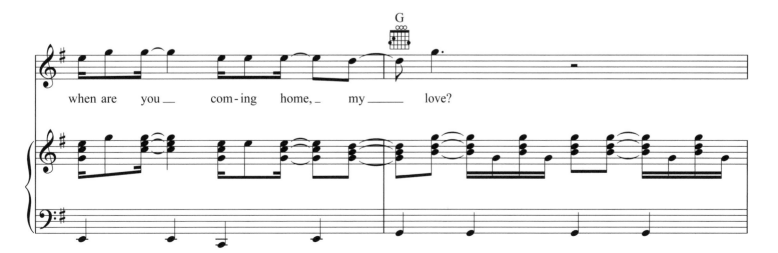

when are you __ com- ing home, __ my __ love?

Well, I've been a - lone __ far too __ long,

when are you __ com - ing home, __ my __ love? My

love. __   Well, I've   love. __

MESS IS MINE

Words and Music by
VANCE JOY

Moderately, with a beat

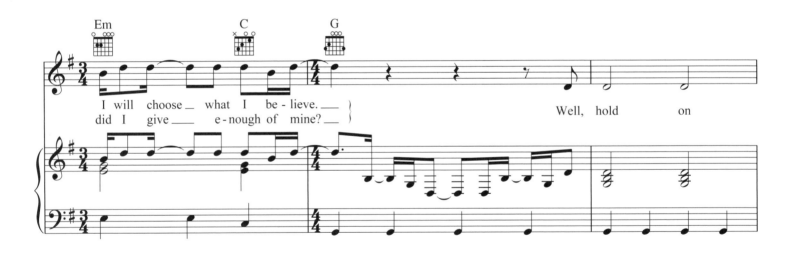

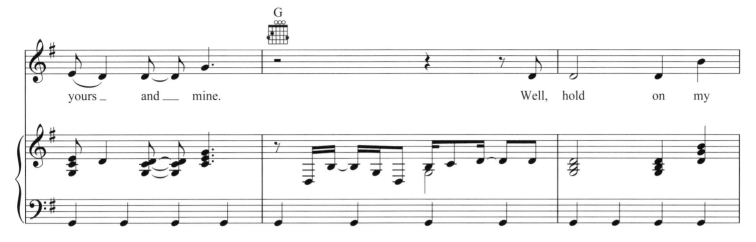

yours __ and __ mine.   Well, hold   on   my

dar - lin'.   This mess was __ yours, __

now __ your mess is __ mine. __

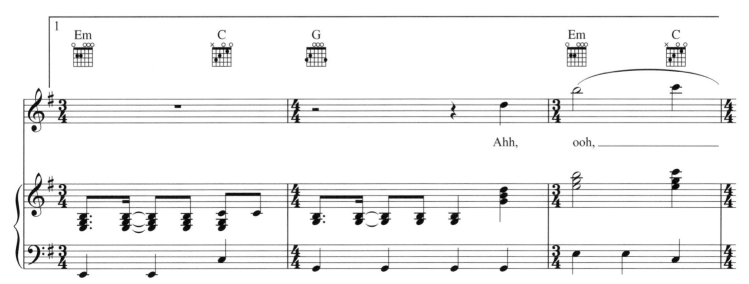

Ahh,   ooh, _____

your mess is mine.

Ooh, _____ your mess is ___ mine. _____

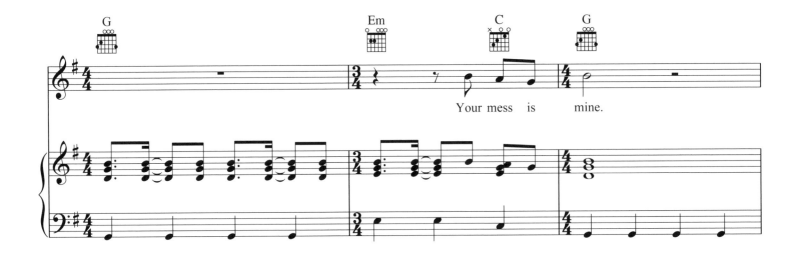

Your mess is mine.

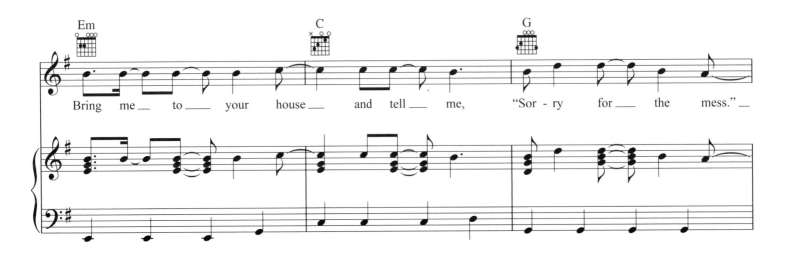

Bring me ___ to ___ your house ___ and tell ___ me, "Sor - ry for ___ the mess." ___

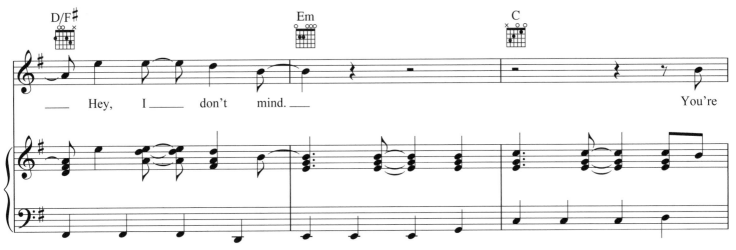

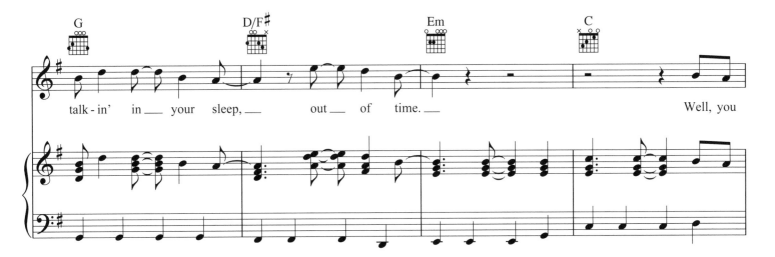

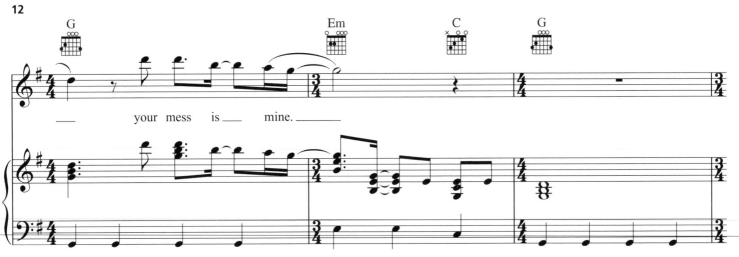

your mess is mine.

This bod-y's yours and this bod-y's mine.

Ooh, your mess is mine.

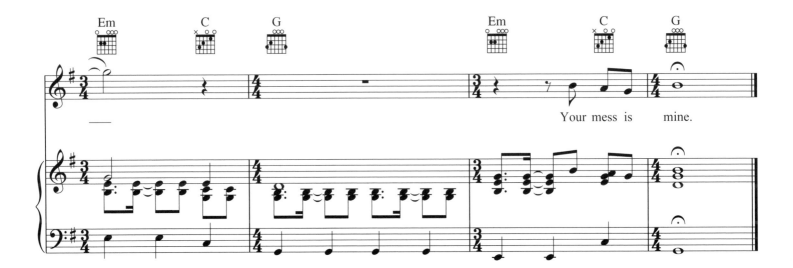

Your mess is mine.

WASTED TIME

Words and Music by
VANCE JOY

Moderate Folk

Why? _____ Why do you _ go
Why do you _ go

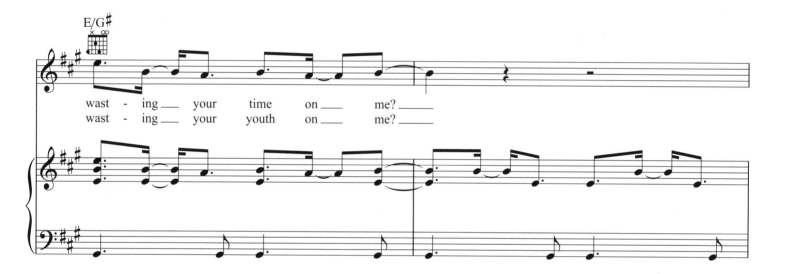

wast - ing __ your time on __ me? _____
wast - ing __ your youth on __ me? _____

You're so beau - ti - ful now,
You're so beau - ti - ful now,
there's
there's

so much_ that's left for you _ now. _____
so much_ time left for you _ now. _____

Oh, yeah, _____ babe.   And why? __
Oh, yeah, _____ babe.   Why? __

__   Why do you_ go
__   We look _ at _ the

flash - ing_ those eyes at _ me? ____   You
fac - es _ on your bed - room wall.

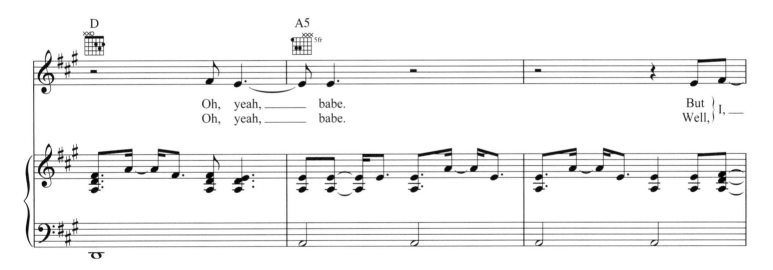

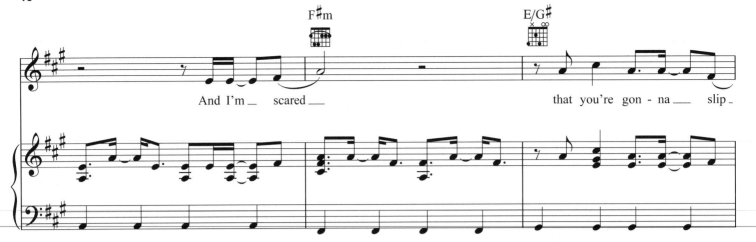

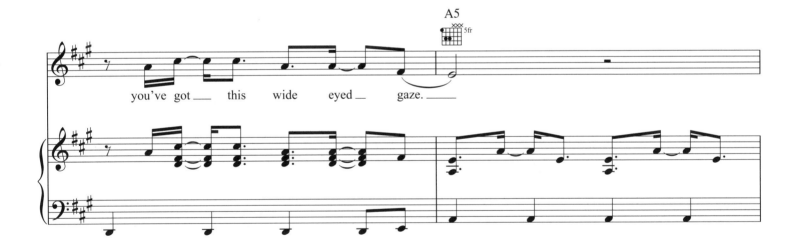

your days. ___   Oh, why? _____

Oh, why? _____   It's the ea -

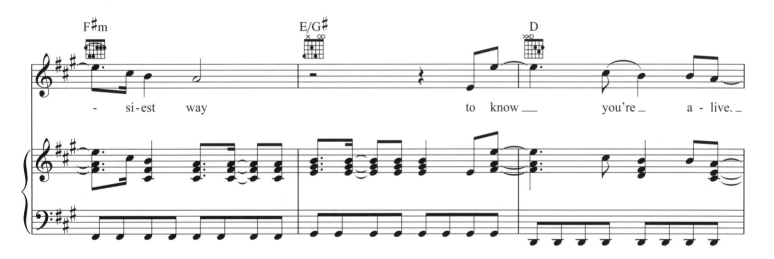

\- si - est way   to know ___ you're ___ a - live. ___

___   And the beau - ty of her, ___   I see her

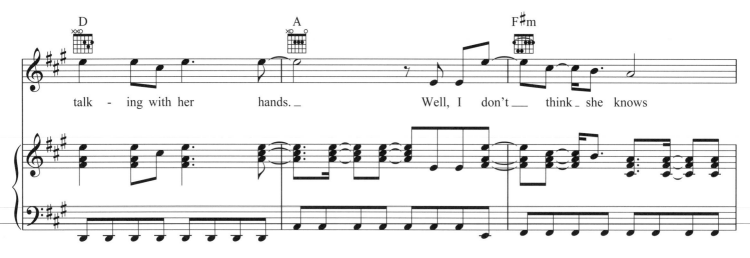

talk - ing with her hands. ___ Well, I don't ___ think ___ she knows

how she changed ___ all ___ my plans. ___ Why? ___

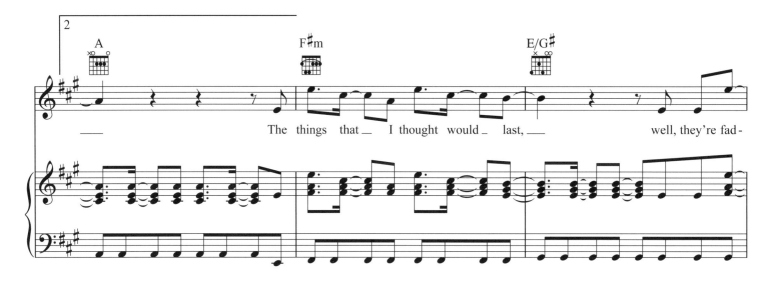

___ The things that ___ I thought would ___ last, ___ well, they're fad -

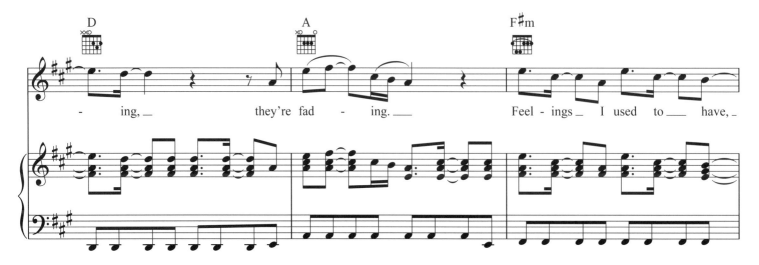

- ing, ___ they're fad - ing. ___ Feel - ings ___ I used to ___ have, ___

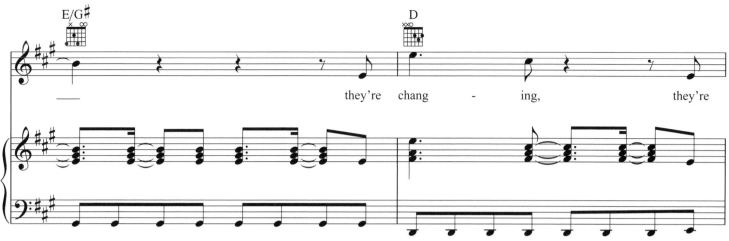

they're chang - ing, they're

chang - ing. _____ The things that _ I thought would last, _

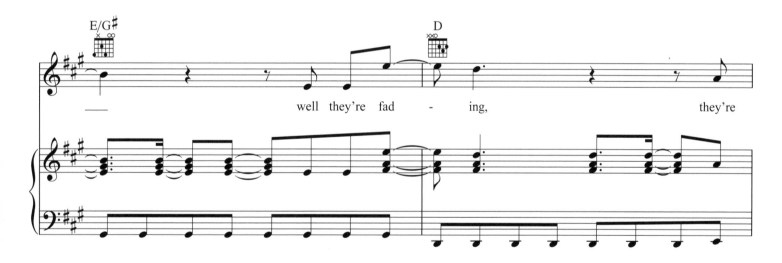

well they're fad - ing, they're

fad - ing. ____ The feel - ings _ I used to _ have, _

they're chang - ing, ___ they're

chang - ing, __ they're chang - ing __ now. __

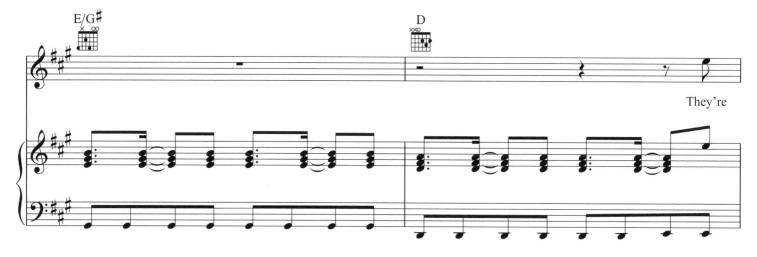

They're

chang - ing, __ they're chang - ing __ now. __

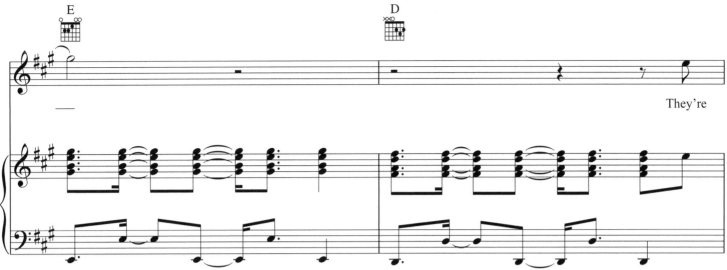

They're

chang - ing, ___ they're chang - ing ___ now. ___

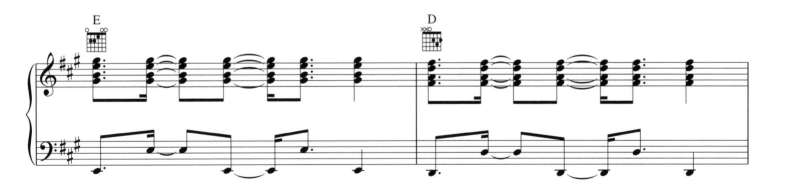

RIPTIDE

Words and Music by
VANCE JOY

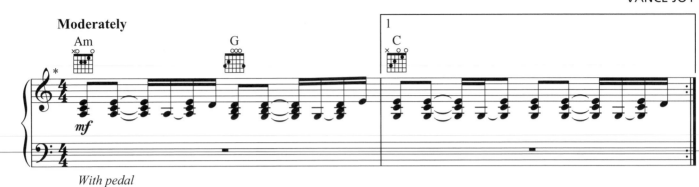

I was scared of den - tists and the dark.___
There's this mov - ie that ___ I think you'll like: ___

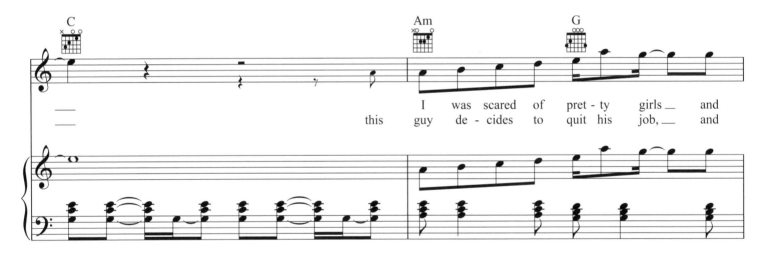

___ I was scared of pret - ty girls ___ and
___ this guy de - cides to quit his job, ___ and

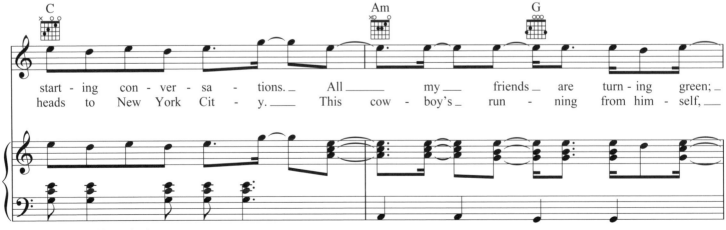

start - ing con - ver - sa - tions.___ All _____ my ___ friends ___ are turn - ing green; ___
heads to New York Cit - y. ___ This cow - boy's ___ run - ning from him - self, ___

Recorded a half step higher.

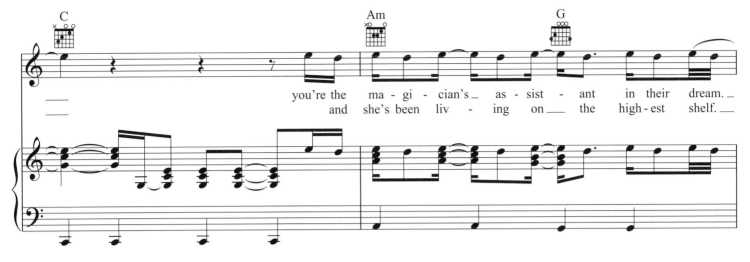

you're the ma-gi-cian's as-sist-ant in their dream.
and she's been liv-ing on the high-est shelf.

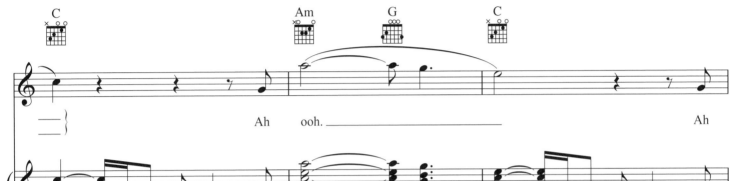

Ah ooh. Ah

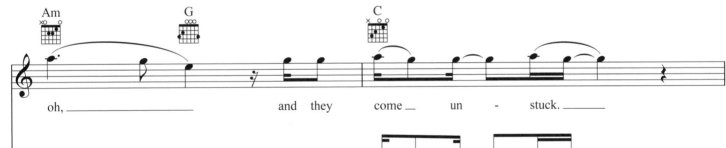

oh, and they come un-stuck.

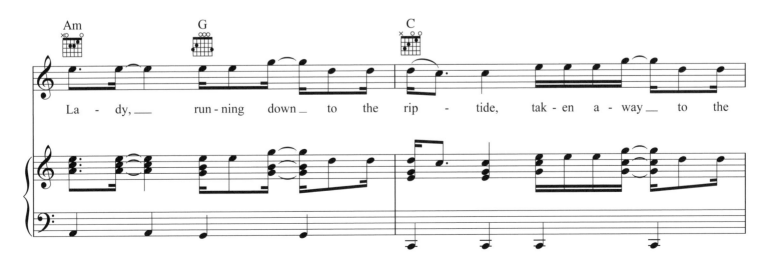

La-dy, run-ning down to the rip-tide, tak-en a-way to the

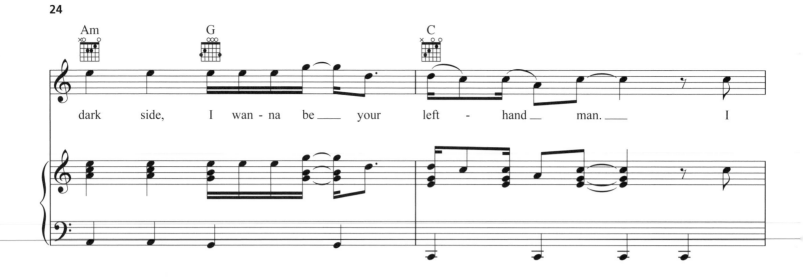

dark side, I wan-na be ___ your left-hand ___ man. ___ I

love you when you're sing - ing that song, ___ and I got a lump ___ in my

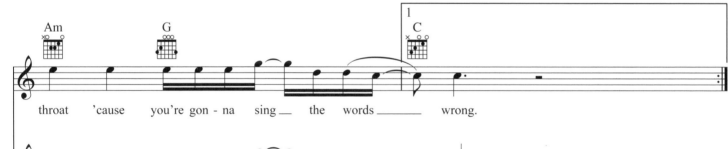

throat 'cause you're gon - na sing ___ the words ___ wrong.

___ wrong.

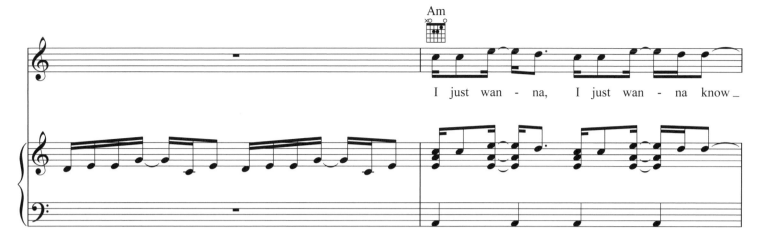

I just wan-na, I just wan-na know _

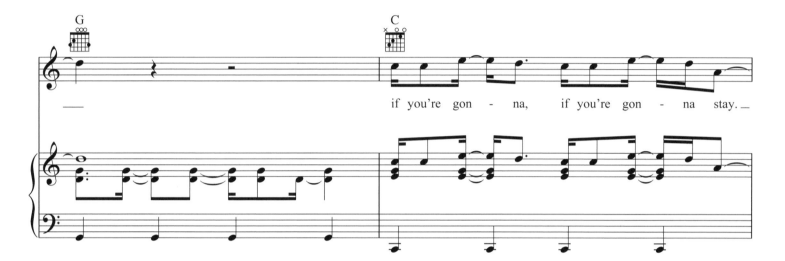

_ if you're gon-na, if you're gon-na stay. _

_ I just got-ta, I just got-ta know; _

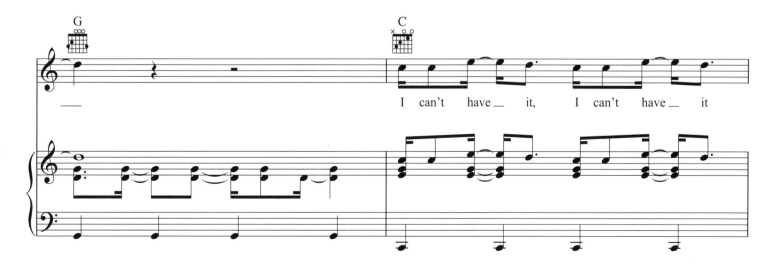

_ I can't have _ it, I can't have _ it

an - y oth - er way. I swear she's des - tined for the screen;

clos - est thing to Mi - chelle Pfeif - fer that you've ev - er seen, oh. ___

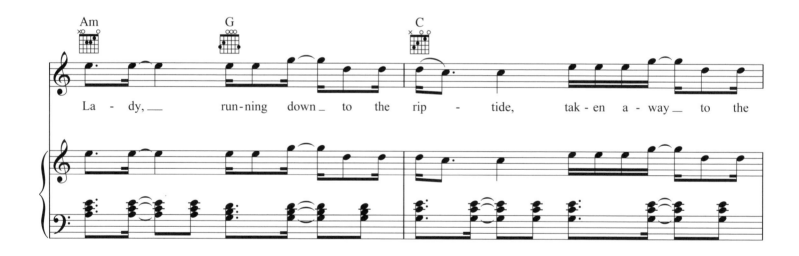

La - dy, ___ run - ning down _ to the rip - tide, tak - en a - way _ to the

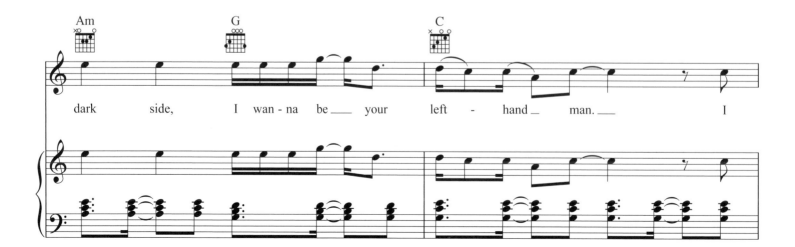

dark side, I wan - na be _ your left - hand _ man. ___ I

love you when you're sing - ing that song, __ and I got a lump __ in my

throat 'cause you're gon - na sing __ the words _____ wrong. Oh,

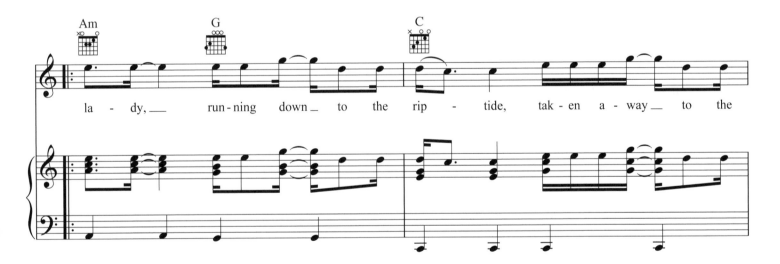

la - dy, __ run - ning down __ to the rip - tide, tak - en a - way __ to the

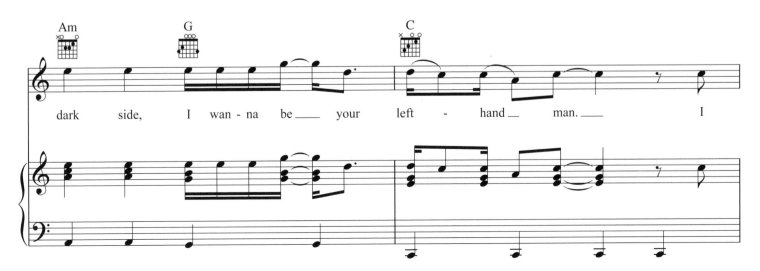

dark side, I wan - na be __ your left - hand __ man. __ I

love you when you're sing - ing that song, __ and I got a lump __ in my

throat 'cause you're gon - na sing __ the words _____ wrong. Oh,

throat 'cause you're gon - na sing __ the words wrong, and __ I got a lump __ in my

throat 'cause you're gon - na sing __ the words _____ wrong.

WHO AM I

Words and Music by
VANCE JOY

Acoustic Pop

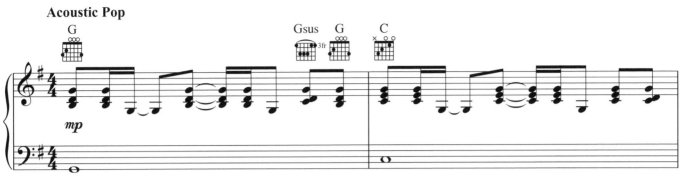

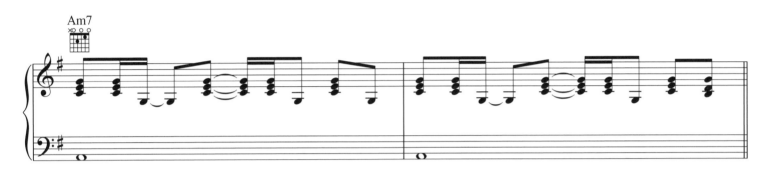

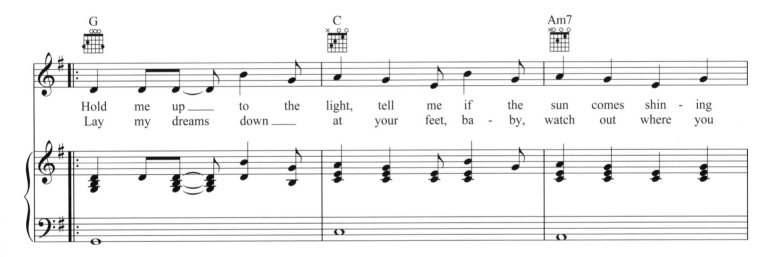

Hold me up ___ to the light, tell me if the sun comes shin- ing
Lay my dreams down ___ at your feet, ba- by, watch out where you

through. And I've got this heav- i- ness in my ___ chest ___ since your
step. And there's no ___ need for us ___ know- ing

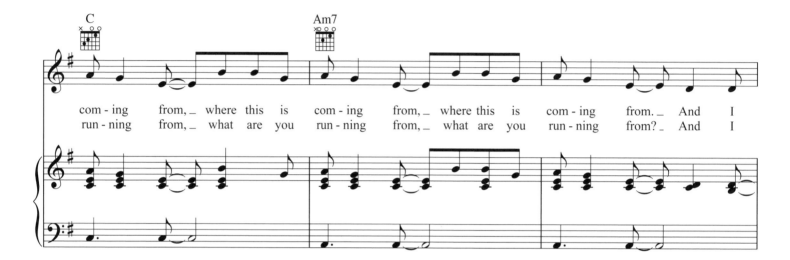

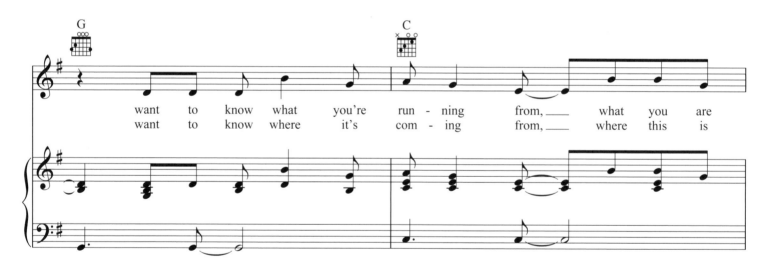

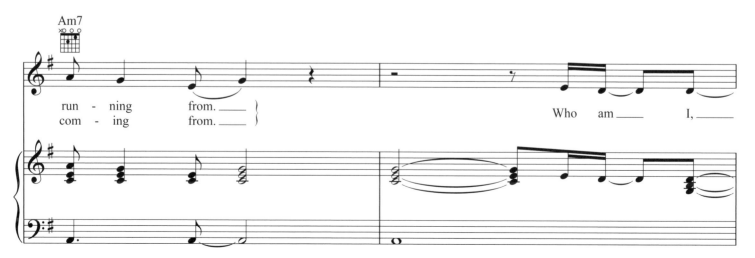

who am ___ I ___ with - out ___

you, with - out ___ you? ___ Who am ___ I, ___

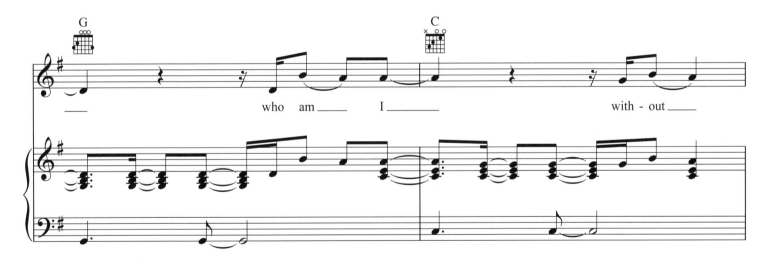

who am ___ I ___ with - out ___

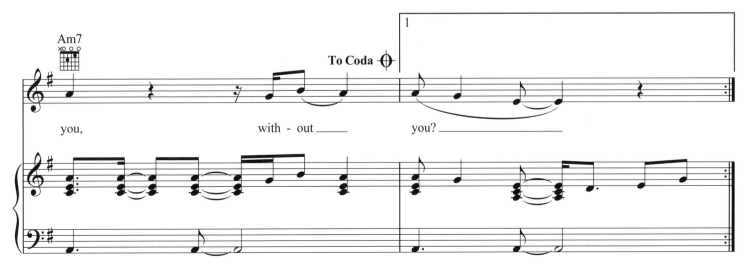

you, with - out ___ you? ___

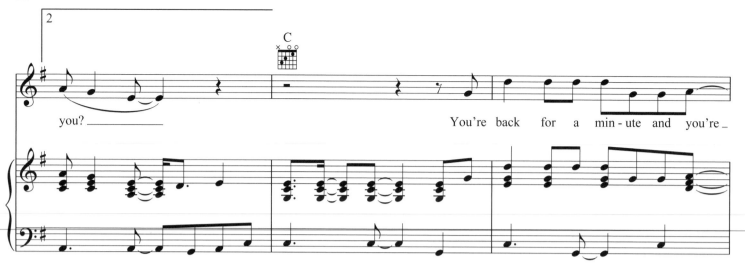

you? _____ You're back for a min - ute and you're _

__ gone and I nev - er know _ how close ___ I came. _ You're

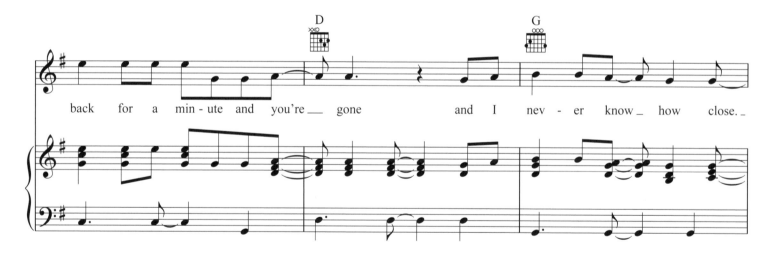

back for a min - ute and you're __ gone and I nev - er know _ how close. _

__ You're back for a min - ute and you're __ gone and I'll

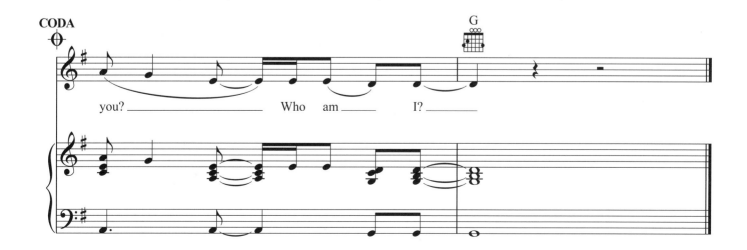

FROM AFAR

Words and Music by
VANCE JOY

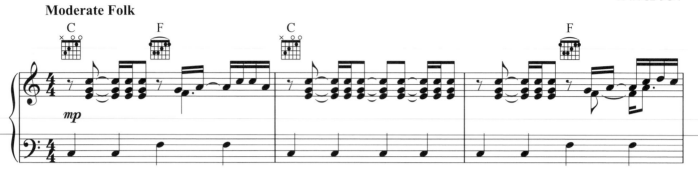

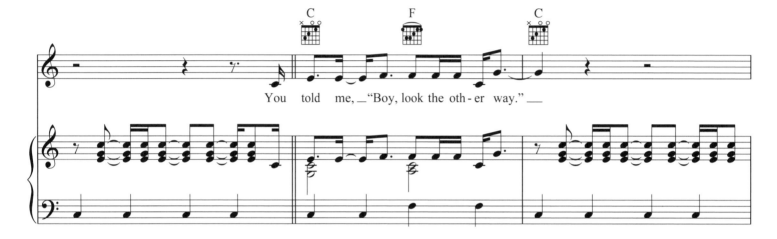

Lyrics:

You told me, _ "Boy, look the oth-er way." _

Told me, "Boy, bite your tongue." _ 'Cause that's not the way. _

Yeah, that's not the way. _ Ahh, that's _ just not the way _ that _ friends be-have.

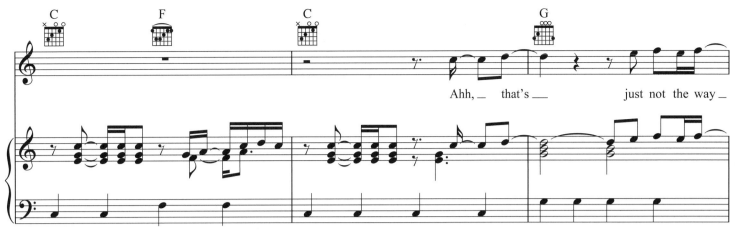

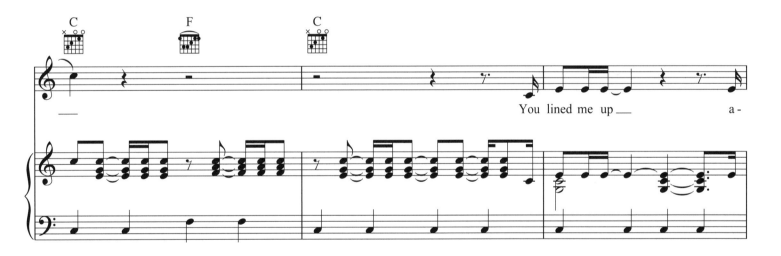

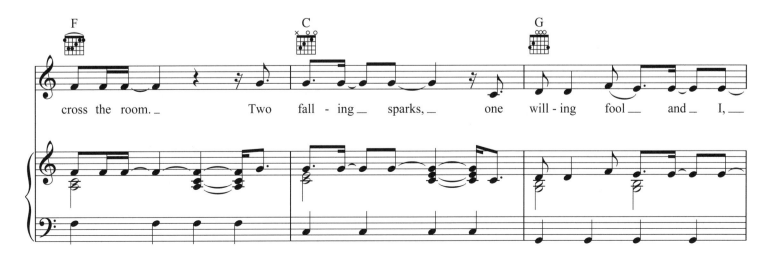

I al-ways _ knew _ that I would love you from a-far.

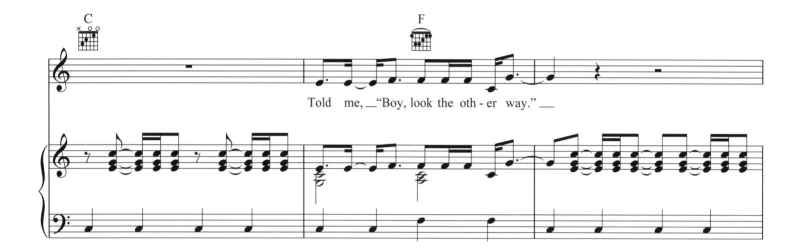

Told me, _ "Boy, look the oth-er way." _

Told me, _ "Boy, hide _ those hands." Well, I've _ been liv-in' on _ the

crumbs of your love _ and I'm starv-in' _ now. _ And that _

is just the way___ that we re-main.

Ahh,___ that___ will be the way___ that we re-main.___

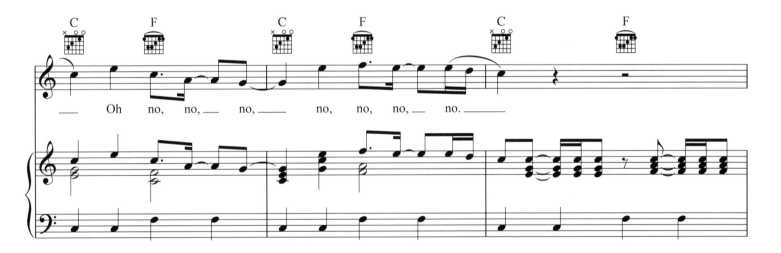

___ Oh no, no,___ no,___ no, no, no,___ no.___

You lined me up___ a - cross the room.___ Two

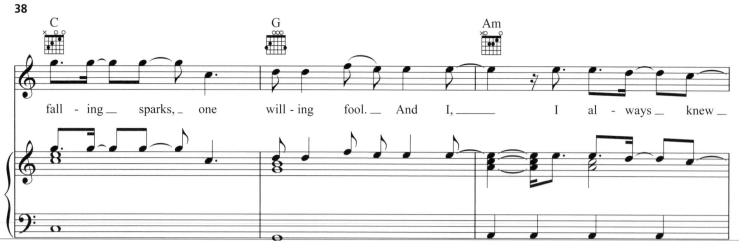

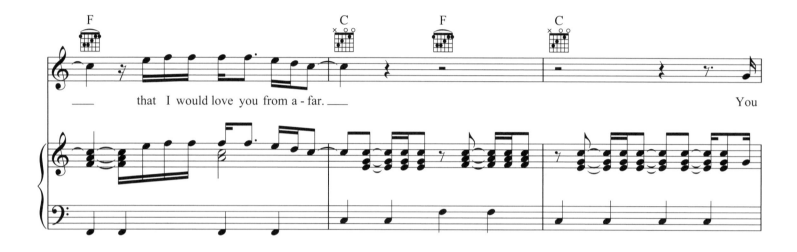

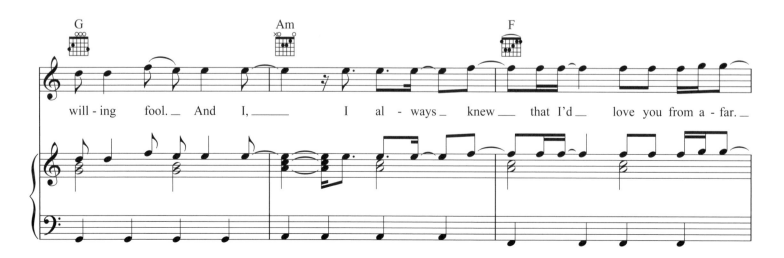

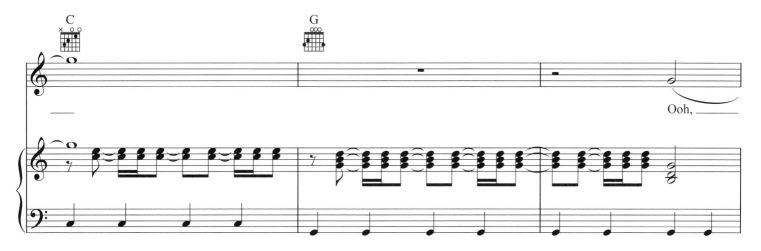

Slightly faster

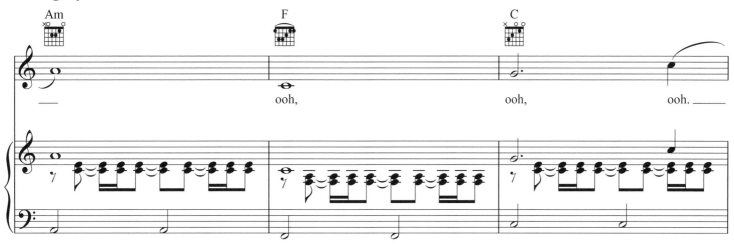

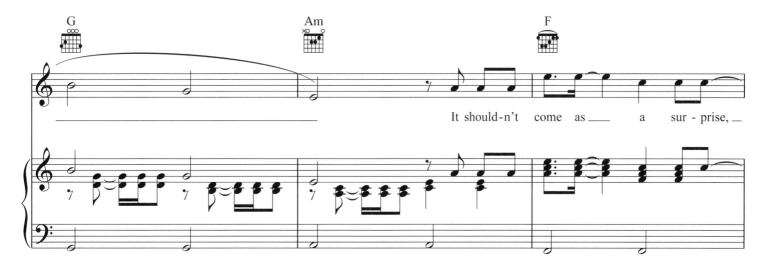

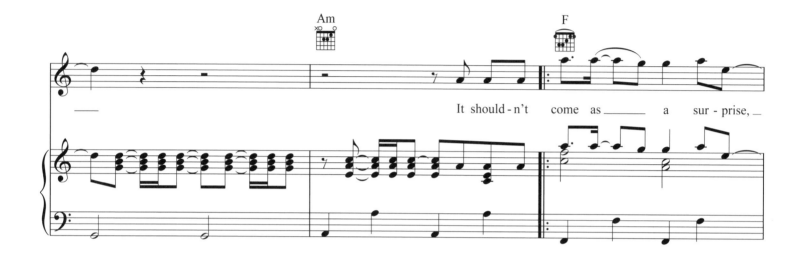

WE ALL DIE TRYING TO GET IT RIGHT

Words and Music by
VANCE JOY

Moderate Folk

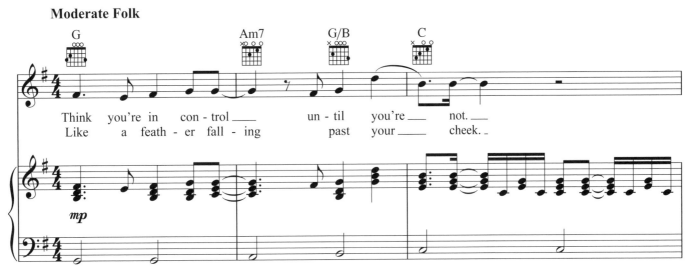

Think you're in con- trol ____ un- til you're ____ not. ____
Like a feath-er fall-ing past your ____ cheek. _

And you're so in love un- til you're ____
Feel the breath of heav- en on your ____

____ not. ____   Find ____ a
____ face. _   We ____ all

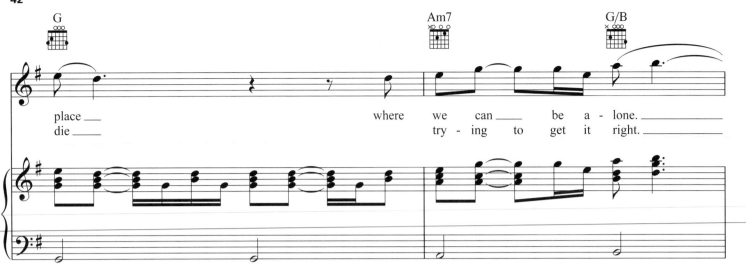

place ____ where we can ____ be a - lone. ____
die ____ try - ing to get it right. ____

____ Find ____ a
____ We're all gon - na

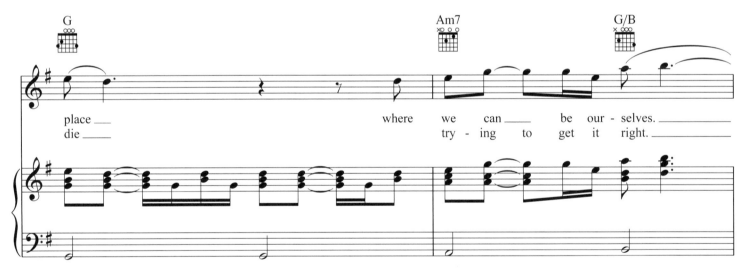

place ____ where we can ____ be our - selves. ____
die ____ try - ing to get it right. ____

So aim _____ high _____

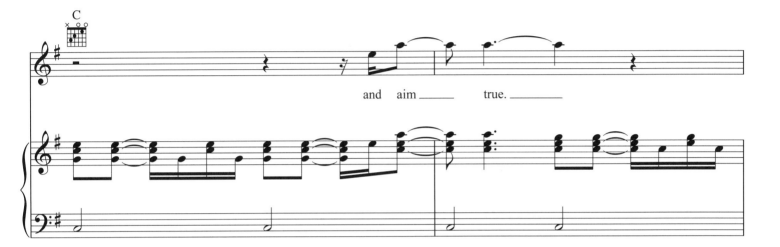

and aim _____ true. _____

Oh. _____

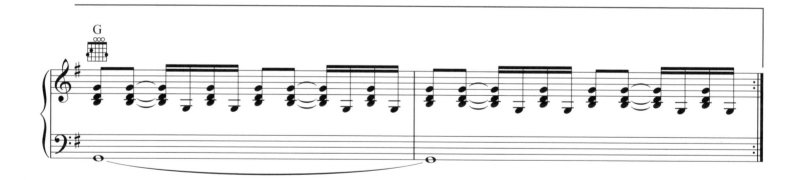

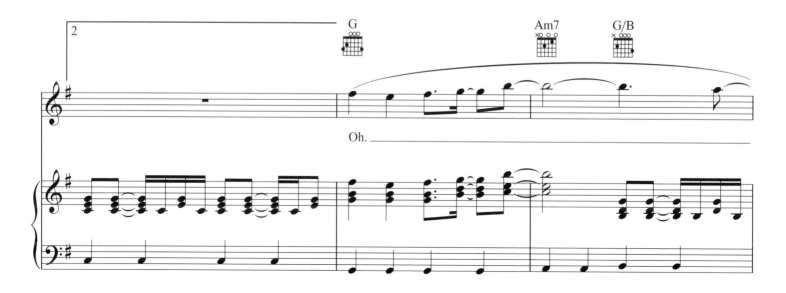

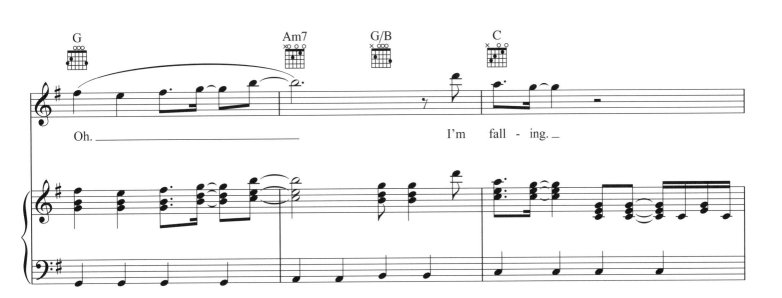

Oh. _____ I'm fall - ing. _

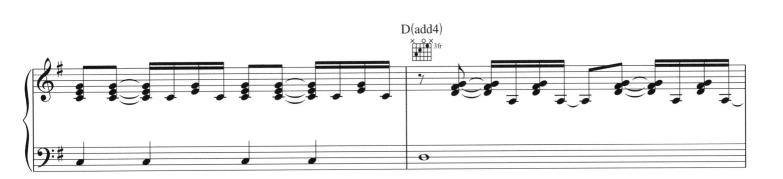

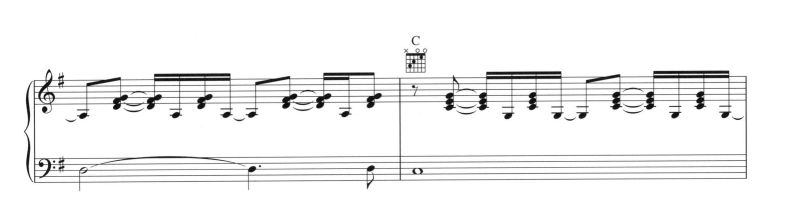

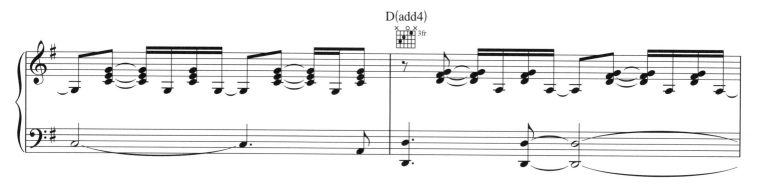

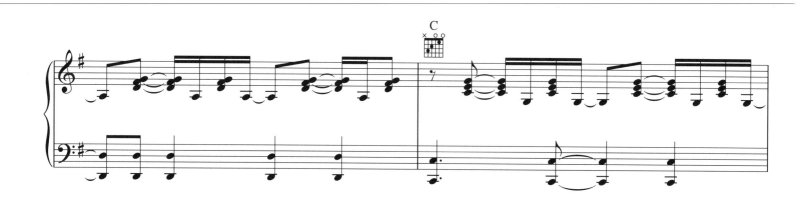

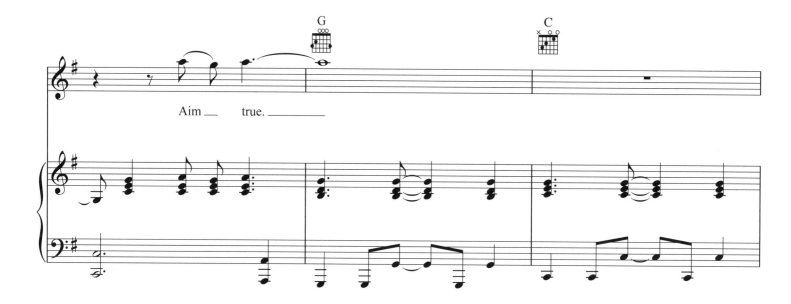

Aim ___ true. _____

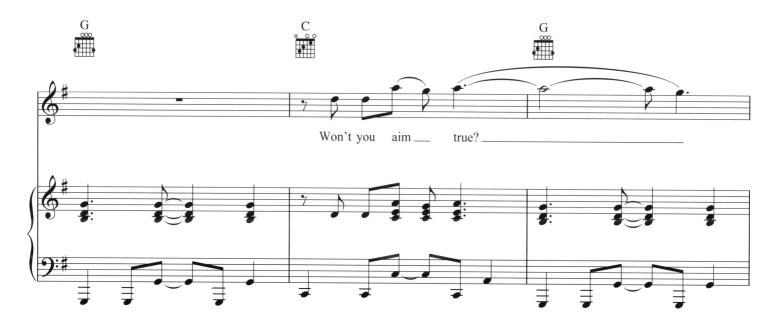

Won't you aim ___ true? _____

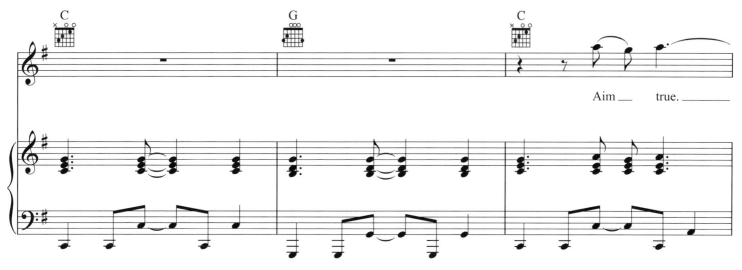

Aim ___ true. ___

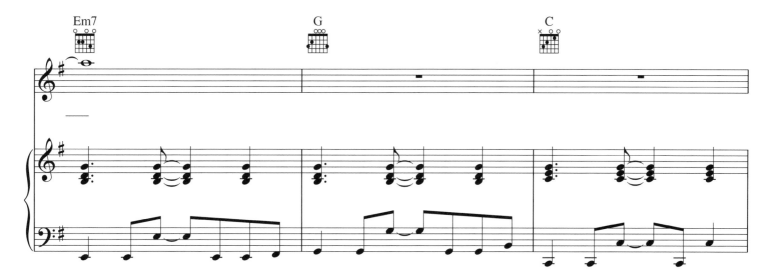

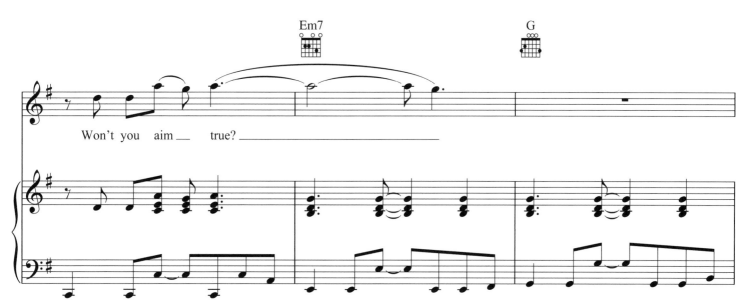

Won't you aim ___ true? _____

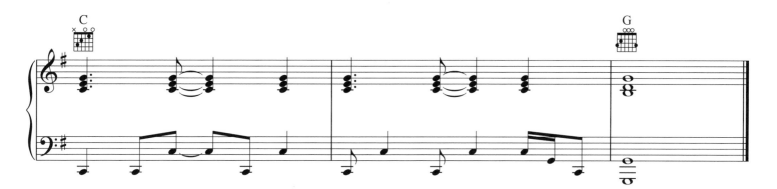

GEORGIA

Words and Music by
VANCE JOY

Recorded a half step higher.

burn-in' up a-gain, I'm burn-in' up. And I, I nev-er un-der-stood what was at

stake. I nev-er thought your love was worth it's wait. And now you've come and gone, I fin-'ly

To Coda

Faster

worked it out. I worked it out. I nev-er should have told you.

I nev-er should have let you see in-side. Don't want it trou-bl-in' your mind.

Won't you let it be? _____ Won't you let it be? _____

Original tempo

D.S. al Coda
(Take 2nd ending)

And

CODA

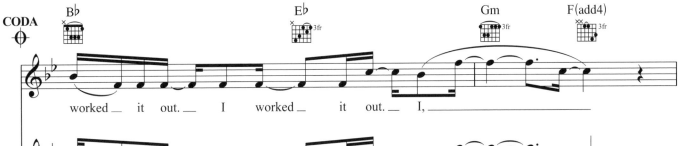

worked _ it out. _ I worked _ it out. _ I, _____

oh, _____ ooh, _____ oh. _____

RED EYE

Words and Music by
VANCE JOY

Acoustic Rock

She don't _____ like _____ small _____
I'm glad _____ that _____ you're still

plac - es,
here. _____

give her high -
Won't you hold _____

- ways and by - ways and don't ____ get stuck in her head. ____
____ up a can - dle, I'm stum - bl - ing in the dark. ____

And it's ____ been _____ so _____
And when ____ I _____ need - ed

long.   And I ____
hope.   I   re -

will read in - to ev - 'ry - thing you don't say. _____
mind my - self that at least _____ I got one thing right. _____

All your _____ si - lent ways. I'm a dog _____
It will al - ways be right.

ly - ing down _____ on a warm _____ bit of pave - ment,

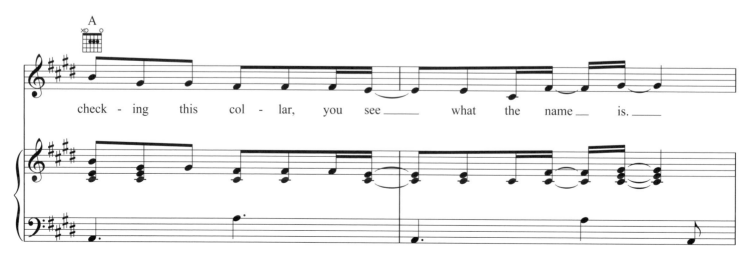

check - ing this col - lar, you see _____ what the name _____ is. _____

Think that it's worth it? ___ Well, I hope that you're right. ___ You're

fall - ing a - sleep ___ on the red ___ eye to - night. ___

And you know ___ that you're look - ing

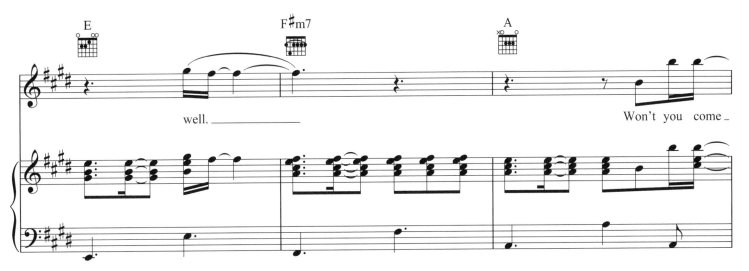

well. _____ Won't you come _

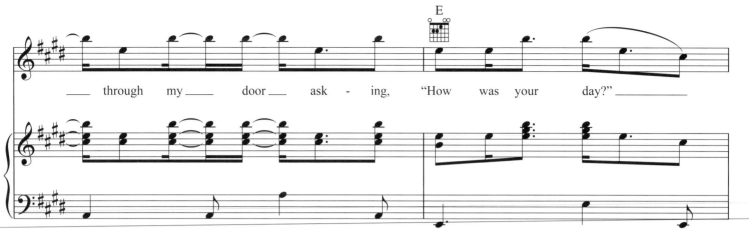

through my ___ door ___ ask - ing, "How was your day?" ___

{ And }
{ Well } you know ___ that I'm still a

dog. ___

And I'm trust - ing my ___ nose, ___ will it show ___

me the way? ___

Won't you

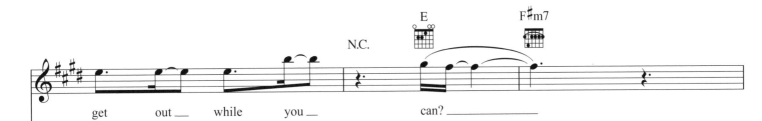

get out ___ while you ___ can? _____

won't you cov - er your eyes _____ if you're

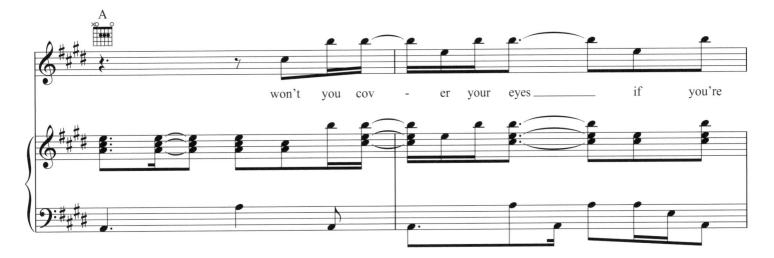

ti - red of ____ see - ing? _____ Won't you

get out ___ while you ___ can? _____

And try sav - ing your - self.

Can we talk in the morn-

FIRST TIME

Words and Music by
VANCE JOY

Moderate Latin groove

Come o-ver to my house, ___ jump in the neigh-bor's pool. ___ It felt ___ nice,
Lead me with your hands. ___ Show me a ___ safe place ___ and I'll ___ calm

___ down. ___ it felt ___ so ___ nice. ___ And it was get-ting dark, ___ you
Yeah, I'll ___ calm ___ down. ___ And can you rec - og - nize ___ the

wrapped your long ___ legs ___ a-round me. ___ I held ___ on ___ tight. ___
look up-on my face? It's on ___ my ___ lips, ___ it's in ___ my ___ eyes. ___ This

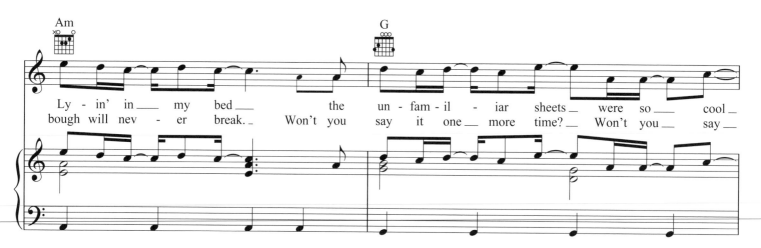

Ly - in' in ___ my bed ___ the un - fam - il - iar sheets ___ were so ___ cool
bough will nev - er break. ___ Won't you say it one ___ more time? ___ Won't you ___ say ___

___ my ___ name, won't you say my ___ on your my ___ my ___ skin. ___ name? ___ This

When your dad - dy called, ___ said you were at ___ a friends ___ and we walked
bough will nev - er break. ___ Won't you say it one ___ more time, ___ won't you say,

the long ___ way ___ home. ___
say ___ my ___ name? ___
Go - in' on ___ my first im - pres - sion,

I re-call __ you wear-in' white. __ There was some - thin' sweet in the air, babe, __

__ that sum-mer night. __ There will al - ways be __ an - oth - er time __

__ for us __ to fall __ in love. __ But it nev - er cuts __ you quite __ as

deep   as that __ first __ time, __ ooh. __   Oh,

you'll find ___ out that the deep - est cut ___ is the first ___

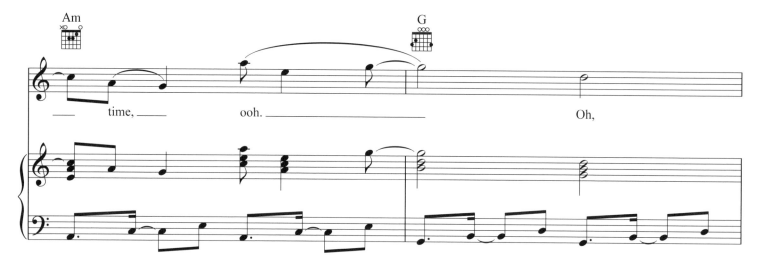

___ time, ___ ooh. _____ Oh,

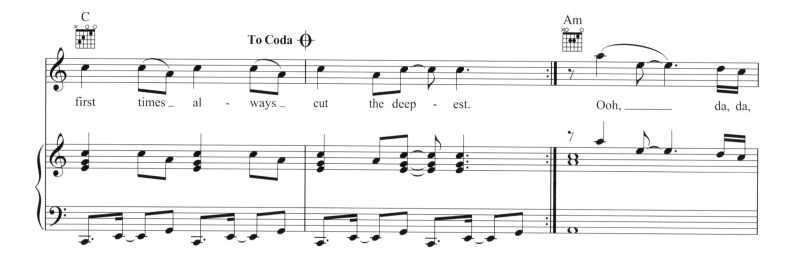

To Coda ⊕

first times _ al - ways _ cut the deep - est. Ooh, ___ da, da,

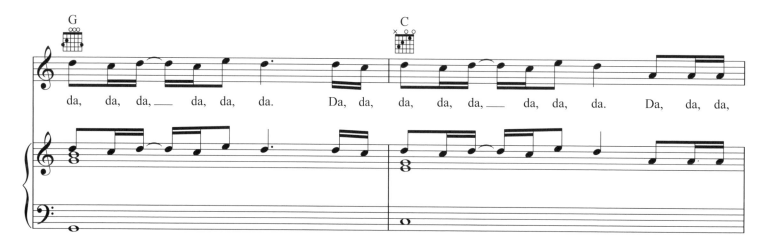

da, da, da, ___ da, da, da. Da, da, da, da, da, ___ da, da, da. Da, da, da,

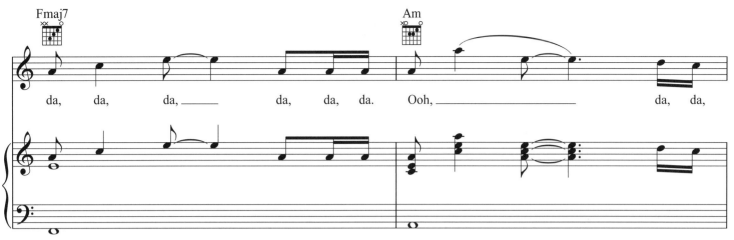

da, da, da, _____ da, da, da. Ooh, _____ da, da,

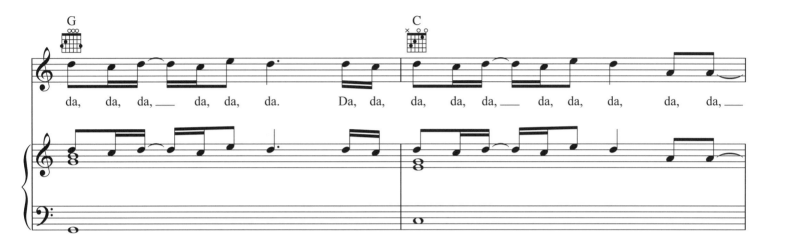

da, da, da, _____ da, da, da. Da, da, da, da, da, _____ da, da, da, da, da, _____

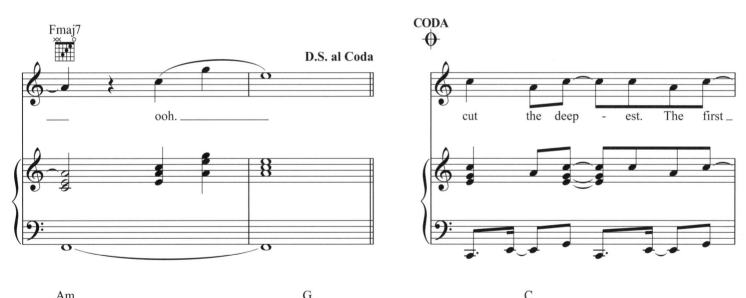

D.S. al Coda

CODA

_____ ooh. _____   cut the deep - est. The first _

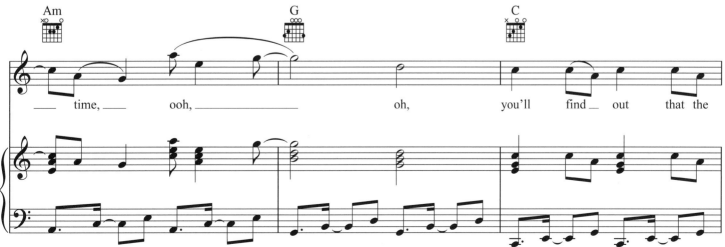

_____ time, ____ ooh, _____ oh,   you'll find _ out that the

deep - est cut __ is the first __ time. __ Ooh, _____ oh,

first times __ al - ways __ cut the deep - est. The first __ time, __

you'll find __ out that that deep - est cut __ is the first __

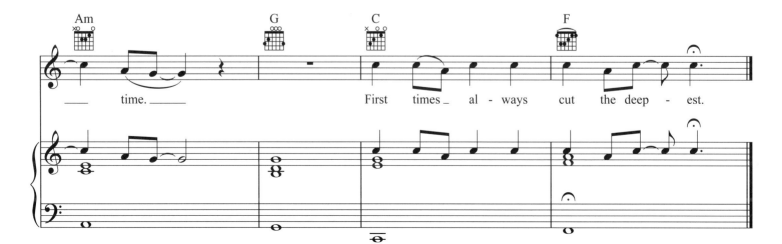

__ time. __ First times __ al - ways cut the deep - est.

ALL I EVER WANTED

Words and Music by
VANCE JOY

Moderate Rock

I was born ___ on a Sat-ur-day. ___ My
that I come on strong. ___ For-

dad, he held me scream-in' in his arms. ___ And he can ___ talk ___ like it was
give me, I just could-n't help my-self. ___ And I have ___ changed ___ but I'm ___

yes-ter-day ___ when I got that ho-ly wa-ter in ___ my eye. ___ It's al-
bet-ter now. ___ And I see you in this new ___ and per-fect light. ___ You're so

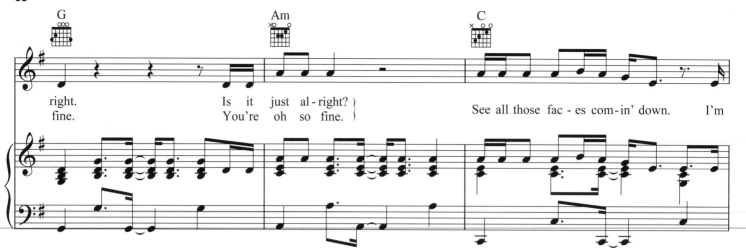

right.
fine.

Is it just al-right?
You're oh so fine.

See all those fac-es com-in' down. I'm

try-in' not __ to let __ them down __ this __ time. __ Babe, __ is that __ al-right? Well,

I can still see the sun __ on the wa-ter. I __ can still feel your sun - light. __ And all __ I ev-er __

__ want - ed __ was time. You know that all __

I ev - er _____ want - ed _____ was time.

And I know ___

Da, da, da, da, ___ da, da, da, da.

Da, da, da, da, da, da, ___ da, da, da, da.   Da, da, da, da, da, da, ___ da, da, da, da.   Da, da, da, da, ___ da, da, da, da.

Da, da, da, da, da, da, ___ da, da, da, da.   Da, da, da, da, da, da, ___ da, da, da, da.   Da, da, da, da, da, da, ___ da, da, da, da.

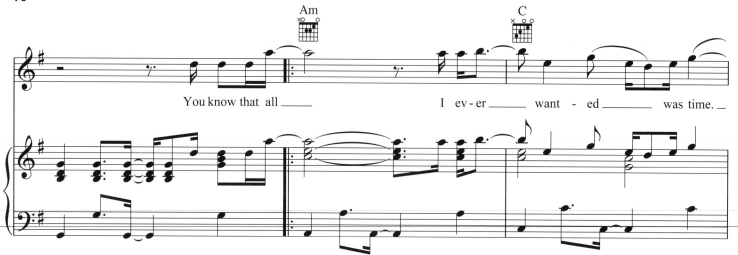

You know that all _____ I ev-er _____ want-ed _____ was time. _____

_____ _____ You know that all _____ we ev-er real-ly _____

_____ need-ed _____ was time. _____

BEST THAT I CAN

Words and Music by
VANCE JOY

Moderate Waltz

Say I don't look much like a lov-er. _____

Does-n't mean that I _____ won't _____ try, _____ set your world _____ on fire

ev - 'ry once _____ in a while. _____ We

* Recorded a half step higher.

lie on the kit-chen floor. ___ Hot air ris-es and it's ___ gon-na be ___

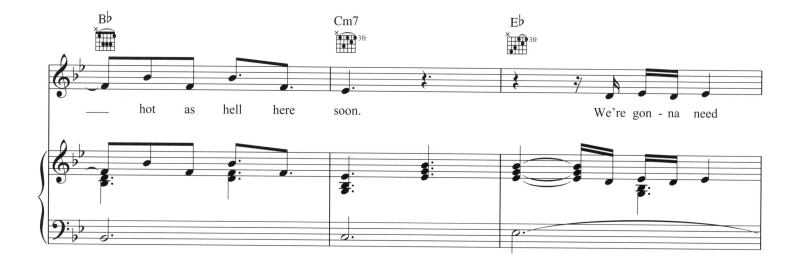

___ hot as hell here soon. We're gon-na need

some re-lief. ___ Sick of leav-in' things half done, ___ leav-in'

things half said. ___ Sick of leav-in'

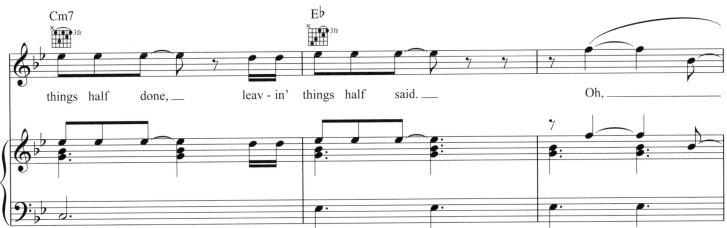

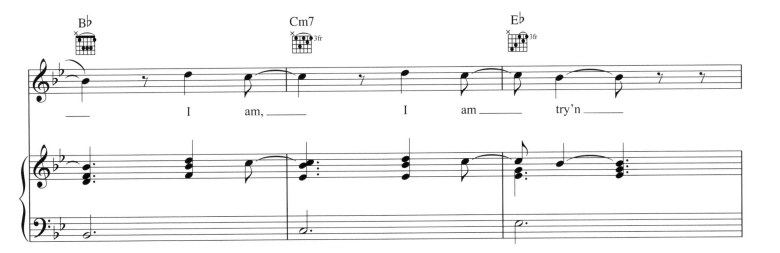

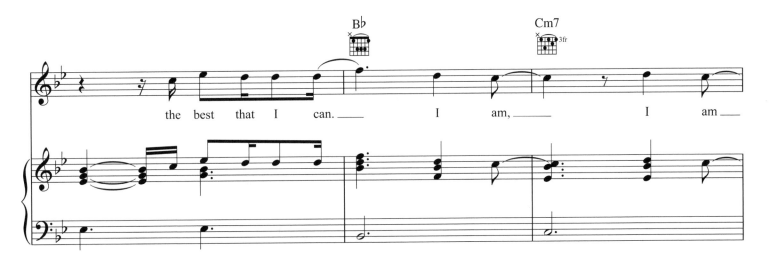

mov-in' on like you do. The road goes as far as the eye can

see. I won't stand in your way. ___ What's the good

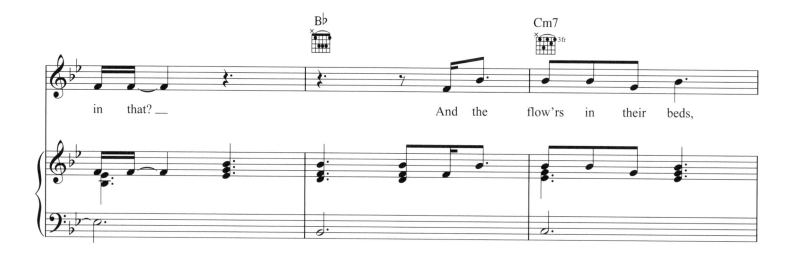

in that? ___ And the flow'rs in their beds,

they're droop-in' and dy-in' and fad-in' a-way. ___

D.S. al Coda

This weath-er's no _____ good _____ for grow-in' things. _____

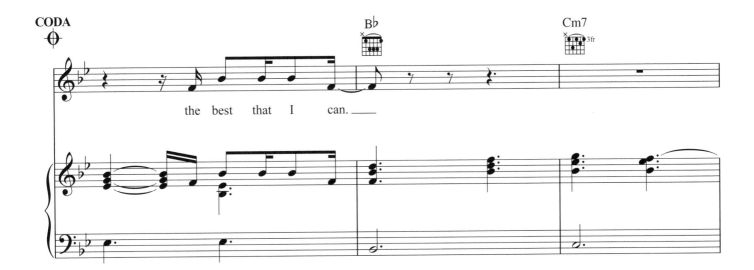

the best that I can. _____

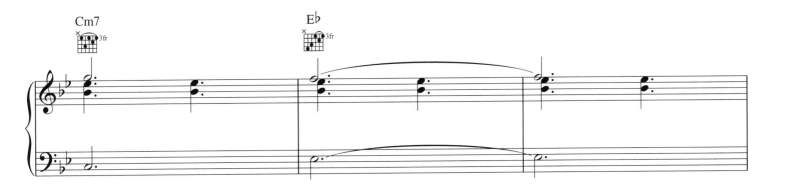

Will you keep mov - in' on like you do? Will you keep

mov - in' on? So will you keep mov - in' on like you

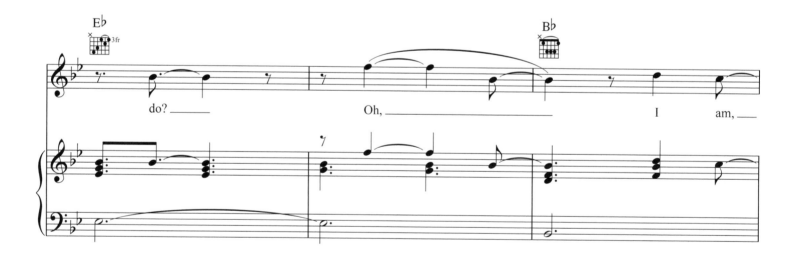

do? _____ Oh, _____ I am, _____

_____ I am _____ try'n _____ the best that I can. _____

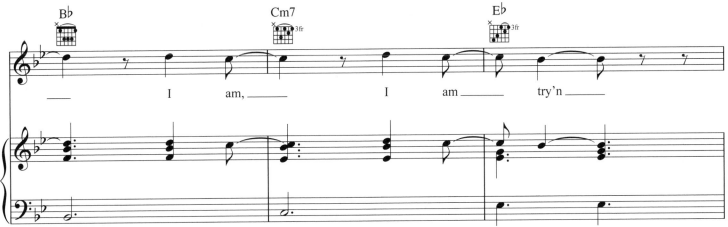

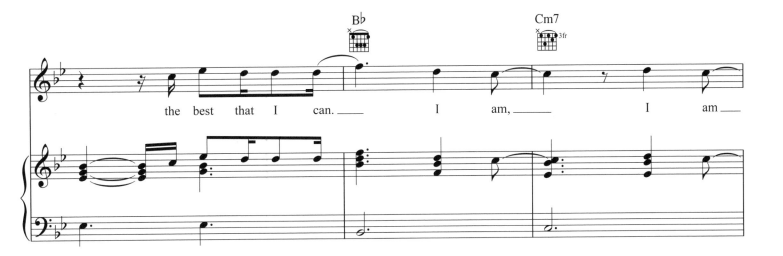

MY KIND OF MAN

Words and Music by
VANCE JOY

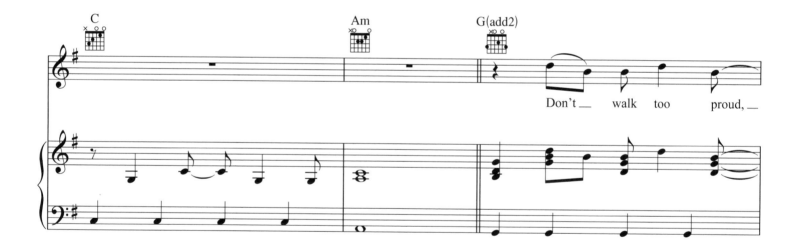

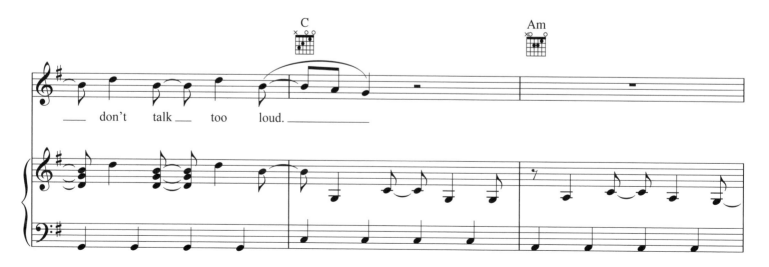

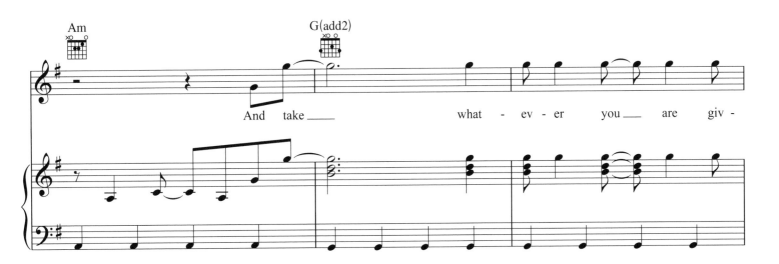

And she said, —

C   Am7   G(add2)

— "You — could be —

C   Am7

— my kind — of man." —

G(add2)   C

And will you do — the best — you can? —

And I could use ____ a lit - tle time. ____

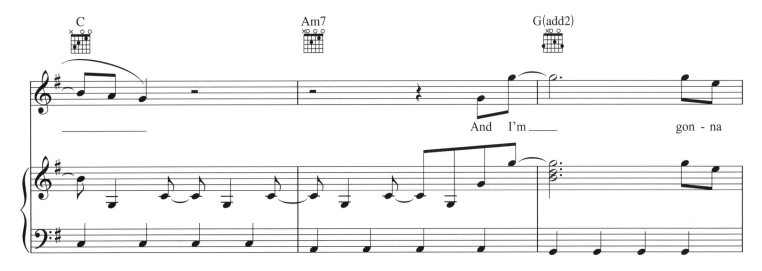

I need ____ to straight - en out ____ my mind. ____

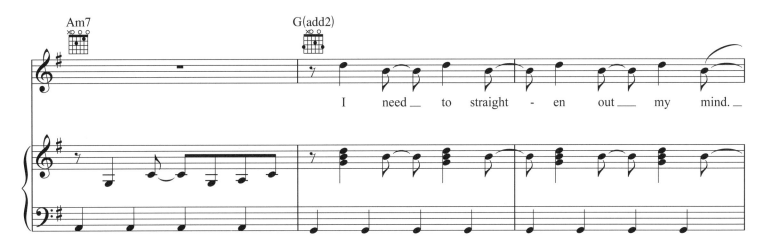

____ And I'm ____ gon - na

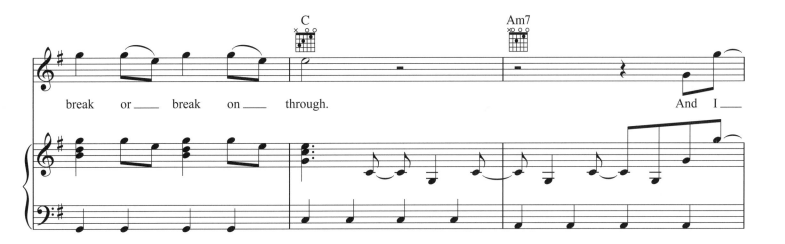

break or ____ break on ____ through. And I ____

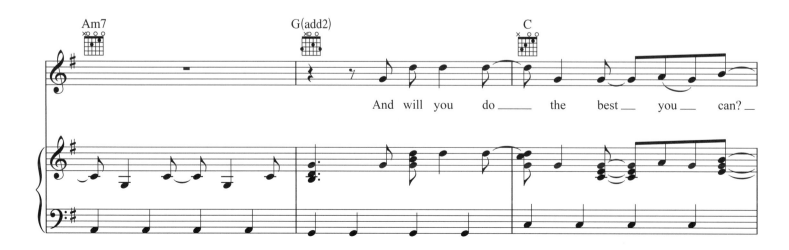

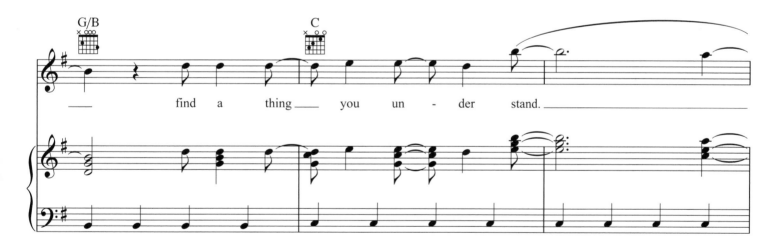

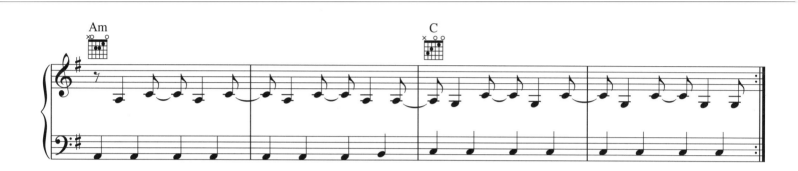

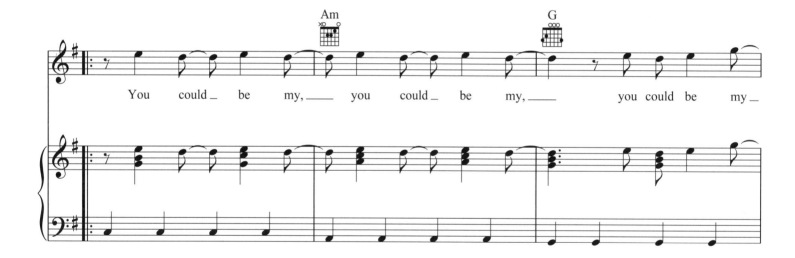

You could __ be my, _____ you could __ be my, _____ you could be my __

__ kind of man. _____ Find a thing ___ that you love, __

find a thing ___ you un - der - stand. ___ Find a thing ___

___ that you love, ___ find a thing ___ you un - der - stand. ___

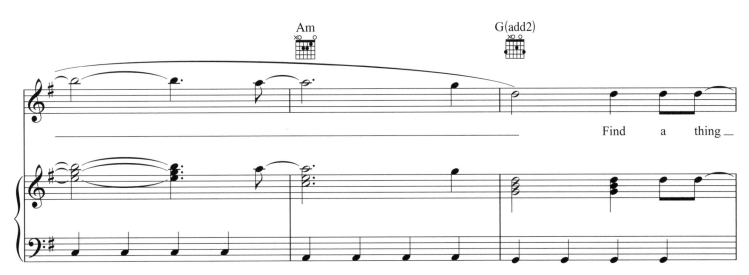

Find a thing ___

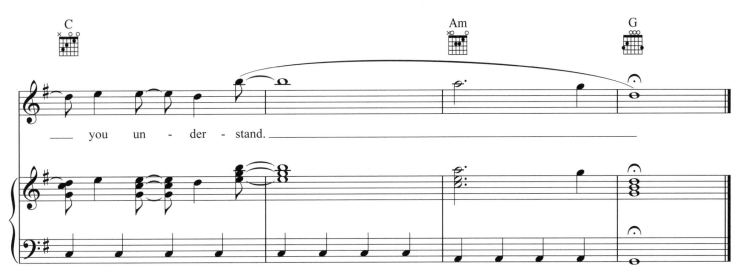

___ you un - der - stand. ___

FIRE AND THE FLOOD

Words and Music by VANCE JOY,
BENJAMIN LEVIN, MIKKEL ERIKSEN
and TOR HERMANSEN

With drive

I was on - ly walk - ing through your neigh - bor - hood,
Since we met, ___ I feel a light - ness in ___ my step.

saw your light ___ on, hon - ey, in the cold ___ I stood.
You're miles ___ a - way but I still feel ___ you.

Anywhere I go, there you are.
Anywhere I go, there you are.

Anywhere I go, there you are.
Anywhere I go, there you are.

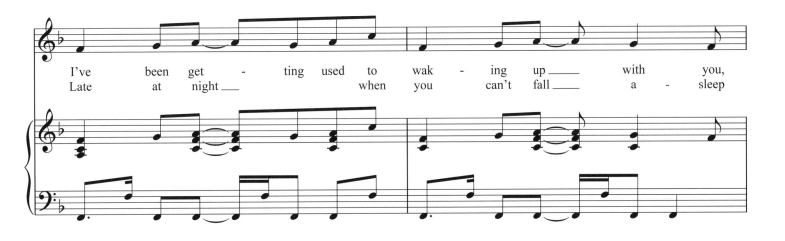

I've been getting used to waking up with you,
Late at night when you can't fall asleep

I've been getting used to waking up here.
I'll be lying right beside you, counting sheep.

An - y - where ___ I go, there you are. ____
An - y - where ___ I go, there you are. ____

An - y - where ___ I go, there you are. ____
An - y - where ___ I go, there you are. ____

There ___ you are, ____ there ___ you are. ____

___ Oh. ____

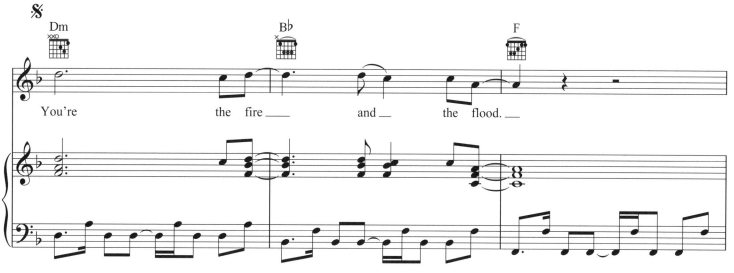

You're the fire ___ and ___ the flood. ___

And I al - ways feel you in ___ my blood. _

___ Ev - 'ry - thing is fine ___ when

your head's rest - ing next ___ to mine, ___ next to mine. ___

To Coda ⊕

You're the fire ___ and ___ the flood. ___

Ah, ooh. ___

Ah, ooh. ___

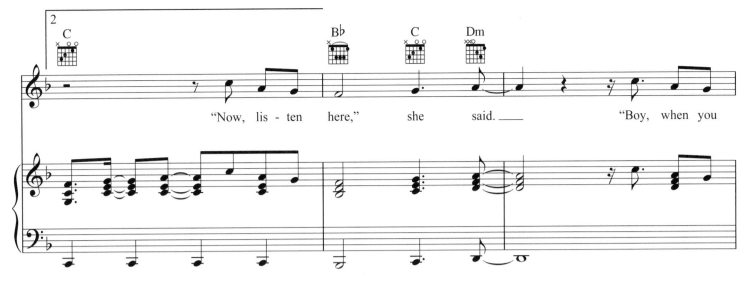

"Now, lis - ten here," she said. ___ "Boy, when you

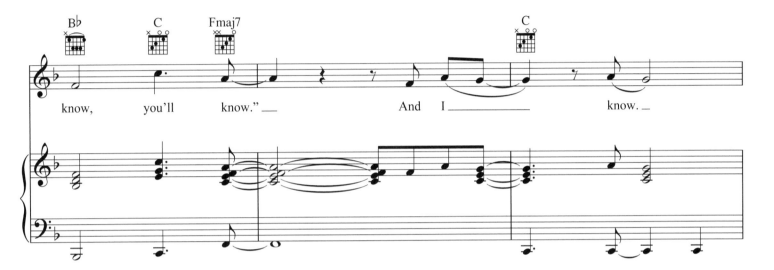

know, you'll know." ___ And I ___ know. ___

Mmm, ___ oh, oh. ___

STRAIGHT INTO YOUR ARMS

Words and Music by VANCE JOY,
BENJAMIN LEVIN, MIKKEL ERIKSEN
and TOR HERMANSEN

like my-self, I've _____ been wait - ing to _____ go straight _____
of what _____ we have. _____ Time is pre - cious, it _____ won't last. _____

in - to your _____ arms, keep _____ me safe. _____
I'll _____ see you _____ when I _____ get back. _____

Ooh, _____ I've been gone _____

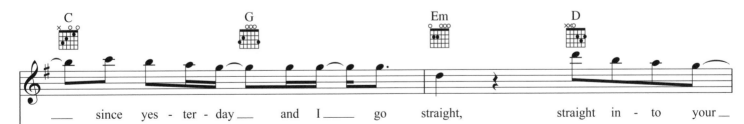

since yes - ter - day _____ and I _____ go straight, straight in - to your _____